HAPPY FATHER DAY

THIS BOOK BELONG TO

- - - - - - - - - - - - - - - - - - -

THERE IS ALWAYS LOVE IN THIS WORLD

SOMEONE......
SOMEWHERE......
IS MADE FOR YOU

About Me

My Picture

_____

_____

_____

_____

_____

_____

_____

What I Love About Myself

_____

_____

_____

_____

_____

_____

_____

_____

_____

About My Father

My Father Picture

_____
_____
_____
_____
_____
_____
_____

What I Love About My Father

_____
_____
_____
_____
_____
_____
_____
_____
_____

About My Mother

My Mother Picture

_____
_____
_____
_____
_____
_____
_____
_____

What I Love About My Mother

_____
_____
_____
_____
_____
_____
_____
_____
_____

Mother and Father Love is PURE

Write Down 5 LOVE QOUTES THAT YOU THINK TODAY ABOUT PARENTS

1. _____
2. _____
3. _____
4. _____
5. _____

Explain How This Will Make You Feel

_____
_____
_____
_____
_____
_____
_____
_____
_____
_____

Today is

Sunday Monday Tuesday Wednesday Thursday Friday Saturday

2
0
1
9

1 2 3 4 5 6 7 8 9 10 11 12 13 14 15 16 17 18 19 20 21 22 23 24 25 26 27 28 29 30 31

I'm feeling _____

_____

_____

_____

_____

_____

_____

_____

_____

I'm thinking about...

My goals _____

_____

_____

_____

_____

_____

_____

_____

To Do List

Check	Task	Deadline
☐		
☐		
☐		
☐		
☐		
☐		
☐		
☐		

To Do List

Check	Task	Deadline
☐		
—		
☐		
—		
☐		
—		
☐		
—		
☐		
—		
☐		
—		
☐		
—		
☐		
—		

30 Day Productivity Plan

M	T	W	T	F

You Must LOVE YOURSELF FIRST

Picture of the day

Notes:

Additional Notes:

Additional Notes:

Checklist

- ☐ _____
- ☐ _____
- ☐ _____
- ☐ _____
- ☐ _____
- ☐ _____
- ☐ _____
- ☐ _____
- ☐ _____
- ☐ _____
- ☐ _____
- ☐ _____
- ☐ _____
- ☐ _____
- ☐ _____
- ☐ _____
- ☐ _____
- ☐ _____
- ☐ _____

Checklist

- [ ] _____
- [ ] _____
- [ ] _____
- [ ] _____
- [ ] _____
- [ ] _____
- [ ] _____
- [ ] _____
- [ ] _____
- [ ] _____
- [ ] _____
- [ ] _____
- [ ] _____
- [ ] _____
- [ ] _____
- [ ] _____
- [ ] _____
- [ ] _____
- [ ] _____
- [ ] _____

Quick Checklist

What Should I Do

- [ ] _____
- [ ] _____
- [ ] _____
- [ ] _____
- [ ] _____

Notes

My Parent Wish List

- [ ] _____ - [ ] _____
- [ ] _____ - [ ] _____
- [ ] _____ - [ ] _____
- [ ] _____ - [ ] _____
- [ ] _____ - [ ] _____

Notes

Achievement

- [ ] _____
- [ ] _____
- [ ] _____
- [ ] _____
- [ ] _____

Notes

Quick Checklist

What Should I Do

- [ ] _____
- [ ] _____
- [ ] _____
- [ ] _____
- [ ] _____

Notes

♥ My Parent Wish List ♥

- [ ] _____
- [ ] _____
- [ ] _____
- [ ] _____
- [ ] _____

- [ ] _____
- [ ] _____
- [ ] _____
- [ ] _____
- [ ] _____

Notes

Achievement

- [ ] _____
- [ ] _____
- [ ] _____
- [ ] _____
- [ ] _____

Notes

 # Health and Fitness
Weekly Checklist

	M	T	W	TH	F	SA	SU
Drink 2L of water							
Workout for at least 30 minutes							
Stretch							
At least 5 servings of fruit/veg							
No eating after 9pm							
Try to get 8 hours of sleep							

Name: _____   Date: _____

Report

QUESTION: What are we trying to find out?

PREDICTION: What do you think is going to happen?
I predict that…

PROCEDURE: What needs to be done, step-by-step?

Weekday To Do List

MONDAY

- [ ] _____
- [ ] _____
- [ ] _____
- [ ] _____
- [ ] _____

TUESDAY

- [ ] _____
- [ ] _____
- [ ] _____
- [ ] _____
- [ ] _____

WEDNESDAY

- [ ] _____
- [ ] _____
- [ ] _____
- [ ] _____
- [ ] _____

THURSDAY

- [ ] _____
- [ ] _____
- [ ] _____
- [ ] _____
- [ ] _____

FRIDAY

- [ ] _____
- [ ] _____
- [ ] _____
- [ ] _____
- [ ] _____

NOTES

- [ ] _____
- [ ] _____
- [ ] _____
- [ ] _____
- [ ] _____

Weekly To Do List

SATURDAY

- ☐ _____
- ☐ _____
- ☐ _____
- ☐ _____
- ☐ _____

SUNDAY

- ☐ _____
- ☐ _____
- ☐ _____
- ☐ _____
- ☐ _____

Notes

- ☐ _____
- ☐ _____
- ☐ _____
- ☐ _____
- ☐ _____

Journal

Date: _____

Topic:

_____

_____

_____

_____

_____

_____

_____

_____

_____

_____

_____

_____

Share picture here:

Name: _____   Date: _____

Report

QUESTION: What are we trying to find out?

PREDICTION: What do you think is going to happen?

I predict that...

PROCEDURE: What needs to be done, step-by-step?

A friend
is someone
who knows
all about
you and
still loves
you

~ **Elbert Hubbard**

30 Day Productivity Plan

M	T	W	T	F

Be
Prepared
For
Anything

Write Down 5 LOVE QOUTES THAT YOU THINK TODAY ABOUT PARENTS

1. _____
2. _____
3. _____
4. _____
5. _____

Explain How This Will Make You Feel

_____
_____
_____
_____
_____
_____
_____
_____
_____
_____

Today is

Sunday   Monday   Tuesday   Wednesday   Thursday   Friday   Saturday

2019

1 2 3 4 5 6 7 8 9 10 11 12 13 14 15 16 17 18 19 20 21 22 23 24 25 26 27 28 29 30 31

I'm feeling _____

_____

_____

_____

_____

_____

_____

_____

_____

I'm thinking about...

My goals _____

_____

_____

_____

_____

_____

_____

_____

To Do List

Check	Task	Deadline
☐		
—		
☐		
—		
☐		
—		
☐		
—		
☐		
—		
☐		
—		
☐		
—		
☐		
—		

To Do List

Check	Task	Deadline
☐		
—		
☐		
—		
☐		
—		
☐		
—		
☐		
—		
☐		
—		
☐		
—		
☐		
—		

You Must LOVE YOURSELF FIRST

Picture of the day

Notes:

Additional Notes:

Additional Notes:

Checklist

- [ ] _____
- [ ] _____
- [ ] _____
- [ ] _____
- [ ] _____
- [ ] _____
- [ ] _____
- [ ] _____
- [ ] _____
- [ ] _____
- [ ] _____
- [ ] _____
- [ ] _____
- [ ] _____
- [ ] _____
- [ ] _____
- [ ] _____
- [ ] _____
- [ ] _____
- [ ] _____

Checklist

- [ ] _____
- [ ] _____
- [ ] _____
- [ ] _____
- [ ] _____
- [ ] _____
- [ ] _____
- [ ] _____
- [ ] _____
- [ ] _____
- [ ] _____
- [ ] _____
- [ ] _____
- [ ] _____
- [ ] _____
- [ ] _____
- [ ] _____
- [ ] _____
- [ ] _____

Quick Checklist

What Should I Do

- ☐ _____
- ☐ _____
- ☐ _____
- ☐ _____
- ☐ _____

Notes

♥ My Parent Wish List ♥

- ☐ _____
- ☐ _____
- ☐ _____
- ☐ _____
- ☐ _____

- ☐ _____
- ☐ _____
- ☐ _____
- ☐ _____
- ☐ _____

Notes

Achievement

- ☐ _____
- ☐ _____
- ☐ _____
- ☐ _____
- ☐ _____

Notes

Quick Checklist

◄ What Should I Do ►

- ☐ _____
- ☐ _____
- ☐ _____
- ☐ _____
- ☐ _____

Notes

♥ My Parent Wish List ♥

- ☐ _____ ☐ _____
- ☐ _____ ☐ _____
- ☐ _____ ☐ _____
- ☐ _____ ☐ _____
- ☐ _____ ☐ _____

Notes

Achievement ☀

- ☐ _____
- ☐ _____
- ☐ _____
- ☐ _____
- ☐ _____

Notes

 # Health and Fitness
Weekly Checklist

	M	T	W	TH	F	SA	SU
Drink 2L of water							
Workout for at least 30 minutes							
Stretch							
At least 5 servings of fruit/veg							
No eating after 9pm							
Try to get 8 hours of sleep							

Weekday To Do List

MONDAY

- ☐ _____
- ☐ _____
- ☐ _____
- ☐ _____
- ☐ _____

TUESDAY

- ☐ _____
- ☐ _____
- ☐ _____
- ☐ _____
- ☐ _____

WEDNESDAY

- ☐ _____
- ☐ _____
- ☐ _____
- ☐ _____

THURSDAY

- ☐ _____
- ☐ _____
- ☐ _____
- ☐ _____

FRIDAY

- ☐ _____
- ☐ _____
- ☐ _____
- ☐ _____
- ☐ _____

NOTES

- ☐ _____
- ☐ _____
- ☐ _____
- ☐ _____
- ☐ _____

Weekly To Do List

SATURDAY

- ☐ _____
- ☐ _____
- ☐ _____
- ☐ _____
- ☐ _____

SUNDAY

- ☐ _____
- ☐ _____
- ☐ _____
- ☐ _____
- ☐ _____

Notes

- ☐ _____
- ☐ _____
- ☐ _____
- ☐ _____
- ☐ _____

Journal

Date: _____

Topic:

_____

_____

_____

_____

_____

_____

_____

_____

_____

_____

_____

_____

Share picture here:

Name: _____   Date: _____

Report

QUESTION: What are we trying to find out?

PREDICTION: What do you think is going to happen?
I predict that…

PROCEDURE: What needs to be done, step-by-step?

30 Day Productivity Plan

M	T	W	T	F

It is not
a lack of
love, but a
lack of
friendship
that makes
unhappy
marriages

~ Friedrich Nietzsche

Be
Prepared
For
Anything

Write Down 5 LOVE QOUTES THAT YOU THINK TODAY ABOUT PARENTS

1. _____
2. _____
3. _____
4. _____
5. _____

Explain How This Will Make You Feel

_____
_____
_____
_____
_____
_____
_____
_____
_____
_____

Today is

Sunday Monday Tuesday Wednesday Thursday Friday Saturday

2 0 1 9

1 2 3 4 5 6 7 8 9 10 11 12 13 14 15 16 17 18 19 20 21 22 23 24 25 26 27 28 29 30 31

I'm feeling _____

_____

_____

_____

_____

_____

_____

_____

I'm thinking about...

My goals _____

_____

_____

_____

_____

_____

_____

_____

To Do List

Check	Task	Deadline
☐		
☐		
☐		
☐		
☐		
☐		
☐		
☐		

To Do List

Check	Task	Deadline
☐		
—		
☐		
—		
☐		
—		
☐		
—		
☐		
—		
☐		
—		
☐		
—		
☐		
—		

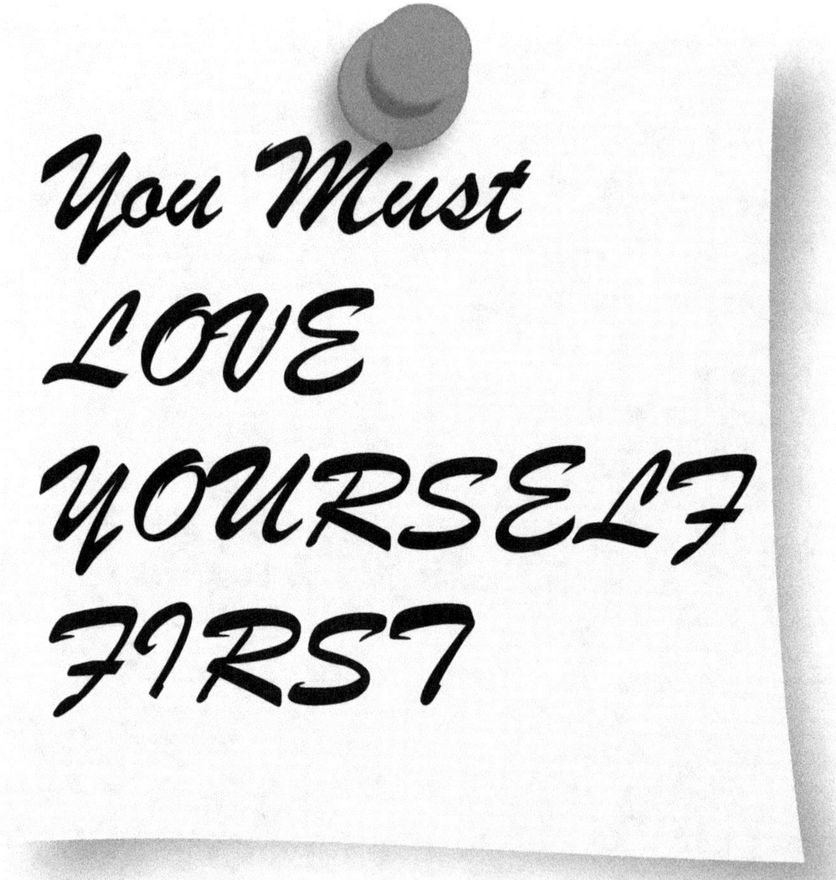
You Must
LOVE
YOURSELF
FIRST

Picture of the day

Notes:

Additional Notes:

Additional Notes:

Checklist

- [ ] _____
- [ ] _____
- [ ] _____
- [ ] _____
- [ ] _____
- [ ] _____
- [ ] _____
- [ ] _____
- [ ] _____
- [ ] _____
- [ ] _____
- [ ] _____
- [ ] _____
- [ ] _____
- [ ] _____
- [ ] _____
- [ ] _____
- [ ] _____
- [ ] _____

Checklist

- ☐ _____
- ☐ _____
- ☐ _____
- ☐ _____
- ☐ _____
- ☐ _____
- ☐ _____
- ☐ _____
- ☐ _____
- ☐ _____
- ☐ _____
- ☐ _____
- ☐ _____
- ☐ _____
- ☐ _____
- ☐ _____
- ☐ _____
- ☐ _____
- ☐ _____
- ☐ _____

Quick Checklist

What Should I Do

- [ ] _____
- [ ] _____
- [ ] _____
- [ ] _____
- [ ] _____

Notes

♥ My Parent Wish List ♥

- [ ] _____
- [ ] _____
- [ ] _____
- [ ] _____
- [ ] _____
- [ ] _____
- [ ] _____
- [ ] _____
- [ ] _____
- [ ] _____

Notes

Achievement

- [ ] _____
- [ ] _____
- [ ] _____
- [ ] _____
- [ ] _____

Notes

Quick Checklist

What Should I Do

- [ ] _____
- [ ] _____
- [ ] _____
- [ ] _____
- [ ] _____

Notes

♥ My Parent Wish List ♥

- [ ] _____ [ ] _____
- [ ] _____ [ ] _____
- [ ] _____ [ ] _____
- [ ] _____ [ ] _____
- [ ] _____ [ ] _____

Notes

Achievement

- [ ] _____
- [ ] _____
- [ ] _____
- [ ] _____
- [ ] _____

Notes

Health and Fitness Weekly Checklist

	M	T	W	TH	F	SA	SU
Drink 2L of water							
Workout for at least 30 minutes							
Stretch							
At least 5 servings of fruit/veg							
No eating after 9pm							
Try to get 8 hours of sleep							

Weekday To Do List

MONDAY

- ☐ _____
- ☐ _____
- ☐ _____
- ☐ _____
- ☐ _____

TUESDAY

- ☐ _____
- ☐ _____
- ☐ _____
- ☐ _____
- ☐ _____

WEDNESDAY

- ☐ _____
- ☐ _____
- ☐ _____
- ☐ _____
- ☐ _____

THURSDAY

- ☐ _____
- ☐ _____
- ☐ _____
- ☐ _____
- ☐ _____

FRIDAY

- ☐ _____
- ☐ _____
- ☐ _____
- ☐ _____
- ☐ _____

NOTES

- ☐ _____
- ☐ _____
- ☐ _____
- ☐ _____
- ☐ _____

Weekly To Do List

SATURDAY

- ☐ _____
- ☐ _____
- ☐ _____
- ☐ _____
- ☐ _____

SUNDAY

- ☐ _____
- ☐ _____
- ☐ _____
- ☐ _____
- ☐ _____

Notes

- ☐ _____
- ☐ _____
- ☐ _____
- ☐ _____
- ☐ _____

Journal

Date: _____

Topic:

_____

_____

_____

_____

_____

_____

_____

_____

_____

_____

_____

_____

_____

_____

Share picture here:

Name: _____   Date: _____

Report

QUESTION: What are we trying to find out?

PREDICTION: What do you think is going to happen?

I predict that...

PROCEDURE: What needs to be done, step-by-step?

30 Day Productivity Plan

M	T	W	T	F

*Love all,
trust a
few, do
wrong to
none*

~ **William Shakespeare**

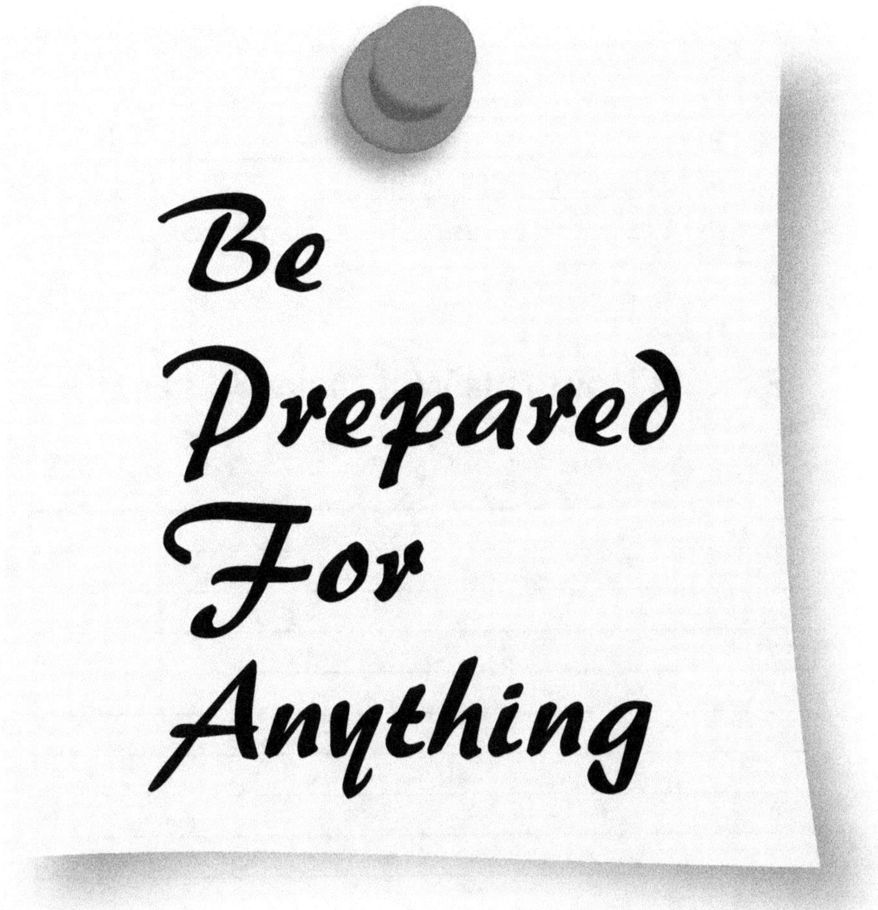
Be
Prepared
For
Anything

Write Down 5 LOVE QOUTES
THAT YOU THINK TODAY ABOUT
PARENTS

1. _____
2. _____
3. _____
4. _____
5. _____

Explain How This Will Make You Feel

_____
_____
_____
_____
_____
_____
_____
_____
_____
_____

Today is

Sunday   Monday   Tuesday   Wednesday   Thursday   Friday   Saturday

2
0
1
9

1 2 3 4 5 6 7 8 9 10 11 12 13 14 15 16 17 18 19 20 21 22 23 24 25 26 27 28 29 30 31

I'm feeling _____

_____
_____
_____
_____
_____
_____
_____

I'm thinking about...

My goals _____

_____
_____
_____
_____
_____
_____
_____

To Do List

Check	Task	Deadline
☐		
—		
☐		
—		
☐		
—		
☐		
—		
☐		
—		
☐		
—		
☐		
—		
☐		
—		

To Do List

Check	Task	Deadline
☐		
☐		
☐		
☐		
☐		
☐		
☐		
☐		

You Must
LOVE
YOURSELF
FIRST

Picture of the day

Notes:

Additional Notes:

Additional Notes:

Checklist

- ☐ _____
- ☐ _____
- ☐ _____
- ☐ _____
- ☐ _____
- ☐ _____
- ☐ _____
- ☐ _____
- ☐ _____
- ☐ _____
- ☐ _____
- ☐ _____
- ☐ _____
- ☐ _____
- ☐ _____
- ☐ _____
- ☐ _____
- ☐ _____
- ☐ _____

Checklist

- [ ] _____
- [ ] _____
- [ ] _____
- [ ] _____
- [ ] _____
- [ ] _____
- [ ] _____
- [ ] _____
- [ ] _____
- [ ] _____
- [ ] _____
- [ ] _____
- [ ] _____
- [ ] _____
- [ ] _____
- [ ] _____
- [ ] _____
- [ ] _____
- [ ] _____

Health and Fitness Weekly Checklist

	M	T	W	TH	F	SA	SU
Drink 2L of water							
Workout for at least 30 minutes							
Stretch							
At least 5 servings of fruit/veg							
No eating after 9pm							
Try to get 8 hours of sleep							

Quick Checklist

What Should I Do

- ☐ _____
- ☐ _____
- ☐ _____
- ☐ _____
- ☐ _____

Notes

♥ My Parent Wish List ♥

- ☐ _____ ☐ _____
- ☐ _____ ☐ _____
- ☐ _____ ☐ _____
- ☐ _____ ☐ _____
- ☐ _____ ☐ _____

Notes

Achievement

- ☐ _____
- ☐ _____
- ☐ _____
- ☐ _____
- ☐ _____

Notes

Quick Checklist

What Should I Do

- [ ] _____
- [ ] _____
- [ ] _____
- [ ] _____
- [ ] _____

Notes

♥ My Parent Wish List ♥

- [ ] _____ [ ] _____
- [ ] _____ [ ] _____
- [ ] _____ [ ] _____
- [ ] _____ [ ] _____
- [ ] _____ [ ] _____

Notes

Achievement ☀

- [ ] _____
- [ ] _____
- [ ] _____
- [ ] _____
- [ ] _____

Notes

Weekday To Do List

MONDAY

- ☐ _____
- ☐ _____
- ☐ _____
- ☐ _____
- ☐ _____

TUESDAY

- ☐ _____
- ☐ _____
- ☐ _____
- ☐ _____
- ☐ _____

WEDNESDAY

- ☐ _____
- ☐ _____
- ☐ _____
- ☐ _____
- ☐ _____

THURSDAY

- ☐ _____
- ☐ _____
- ☐ _____
- ☐ _____
- ☐ _____

FRIDAY

- ☐ _____
- ☐ _____
- ☐ _____
- ☐ _____
- ☐ _____

NOTES

- ☐ _____
- ☐ _____
- ☐ _____
- ☐ _____
- ☐ _____

Weekly To Do List

SATURDAY

- ☐ _____
- ☐ _____
- ☐ _____
- ☐ _____
- ☐ _____

SUNDAY

- ☐ _____
- ☐ _____
- ☐ _____
- ☐ _____
- ☐ _____

Notes

- ☐ _____
- ☐ _____
- ☐ _____
- ☐ _____
- ☐ _____

Journal

Date: _____

Topic:

_____

_____

_____

_____

_____

_____

_____

_____

_____

_____

_____

_____

_____

Share picture here:

Name: _____   Date: _____

Report

QUESTION: What are we trying to find out?

PREDICTION: What do you think is going to happen?
I predict that…

PROCEDURE: What needs to be done, step-by-step?

30 Day Productivity Plan

M	T	W	T	F

Being deeply
loved by
someone gives
you strength,
while loving
someone
deeply gives
you courage

~ Lao Tzu

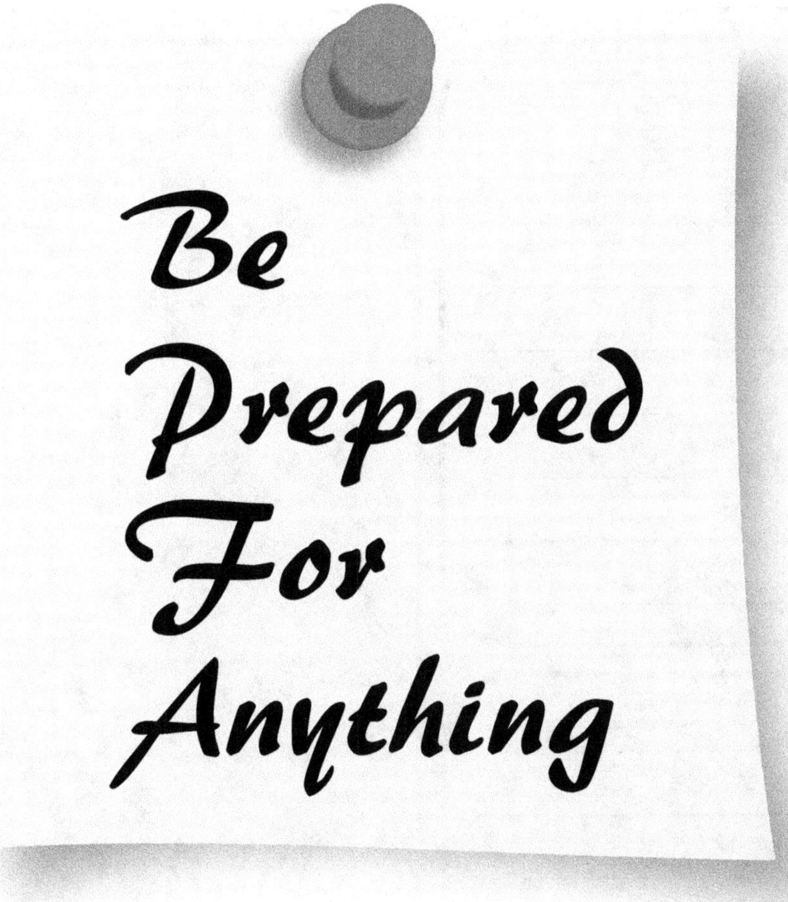
Be
Prepared
For
Anything

Today is

Sunday   Monday   Tuesday   Wednesday   Thursday   Friday   Saturday

2019

1 2 3 4 5 6 7 8 9 10 11 12 13 14 15 16 17 18 19 20 21 22 23 24 25 26 27 28 29 30 31

I'm feeling _____

_____

_____

_____

_____

_____

_____

_____

I'm thinking about...

My goals _____

_____

_____

_____

_____

_____

_____

_____

Write Down 5 LOVE QOUTES
THAT YOU THINK TODAY ABOUT
PARENTS

1. _____
2. _____
3. _____
4. _____
5. _____

Explain How This Will Make You Feel

_____
_____
_____
_____
_____
_____
_____
_____
_____
_____

To Do List

Check	Task	Deadline
☐		
—		
☐		
—		
☐		
—		
☐		
—		
☐		
—		
☐		
—		
☐		
—		
☐		
—		

To Do List

Check	Task	Deadline
☐		
—		
☐		
—		
☐		
—		
☐		
—		
☐		
—		
☐		
—		
☐		
—		
☐		
—		

You Must
LOVE
YOURSELF
FIRST

Picture of the day

Notes:

_____

_____

_____

_____

_____

_____

_____

Additional Notes:

Additional Notes:

Checklist

- ☐ _____
- ☐ _____
- ☐ _____
- ☐ _____
- ☐ _____
- ☐ _____
- ☐ _____
- ☐ _____
- ☐ _____
- ☐ _____
- ☐ _____
- ☐ _____
- ☐ _____
- ☐ _____
- ☐ _____
- ☐ _____
- ☐ _____
- ☐ _____
- ☐ _____
- ☐ _____

Checklist

- [ ] _____
- [ ] _____
- [ ] _____
- [ ] _____
- [ ] _____
- [ ] _____
- [ ] _____
- [ ] _____
- [ ] _____
- [ ] _____
- [ ] _____
- [ ] _____
- [ ] _____
- [ ] _____
- [ ] _____
- [ ] _____
- [ ] _____
- [ ] _____
- [ ] _____
- [ ] _____

 # Health and Fitness
Weekly Checklist

	M	T	W	TH	F	SA	SU
Drink 2L of water							
Workout for at least 30 minutes							
Stretch							
At least 5 servings of fruit/veg							
No eating after 9pm							
Try to get 8 hours of sleep							

Quick Checklist

What Should I Do

- [ ] _____
- [ ] _____
- [ ] _____
- [ ] _____
- [ ] _____

Notes

♥ My Parent Wish List ♥

- [ ] _____ [ ] _____
- [ ] _____ [ ] _____
- [ ] _____ [ ] _____
- [ ] _____ [ ] _____
- [ ] _____ [ ] _____

Notes

Achievement

- [ ] _____
- [ ] _____
- [ ] _____
- [ ] _____
- [ ] _____

Notes

Quick Checklist

What Should I Do

- [ ] _____
- [ ] _____
- [ ] _____
- [ ] _____
- [ ] _____

Notes

My Parent Wish List

- [ ] _____
- [ ] _____
- [ ] _____
- [ ] _____
- [ ] _____

- [ ] _____
- [ ] _____
- [ ] _____
- [ ] _____
- [ ] _____

Notes

Achievement

- [ ] _____
- [ ] _____
- [ ] _____
- [ ] _____
- [ ] _____

Notes

Weekday To Do List

MONDAY

- [ ] _____
- [ ] _____
- [ ] _____
- [ ] _____
- [ ] _____

TUESDAY

- [ ] _____
- [ ] _____
- [ ] _____
- [ ] _____
- [ ] _____

WEDNESDAY

- [ ] _____
- [ ] _____
- [ ] _____
- [ ] _____
- [ ] _____

THURSDAY

- [ ] _____
- [ ] _____
- [ ] _____
- [ ] _____
- [ ] _____

FRIDAY

- [ ] _____
- [ ] _____
- [ ] _____
- [ ] _____
- [ ] _____

NOTES

- [ ] _____
- [ ] _____
- [ ] _____
- [ ] _____
- [ ] _____

Weekly To Do List

SATURDAY

- ☐ _____
- ☐ _____
- ☐ _____
- ☐ _____
- ☐ _____

SUNDAY

- ☐ _____
- ☐ _____
- ☐ _____
- ☐ _____
- ☐ _____

Notes

- ☐ _____
- ☐ _____
- ☐ _____
- ☐ _____
- ☐ _____

Journal

Date: _____

Topic:

_____

_____

_____

_____

_____

_____

_____

_____

_____

_____

_____

_____

Share picture here:

Name: _____   Date: _____

Report

QUESTION: What are we trying to find out?

PREDICTION: What do you think is going to happen?
I predict that...

PROCEDURE: What needs to be done, step-by-step?

30 Day Productivity Plan

M	T	W	T	F

Love is like the wind, you can't see it but you can feel it.

~ **Nicholas Sparks**

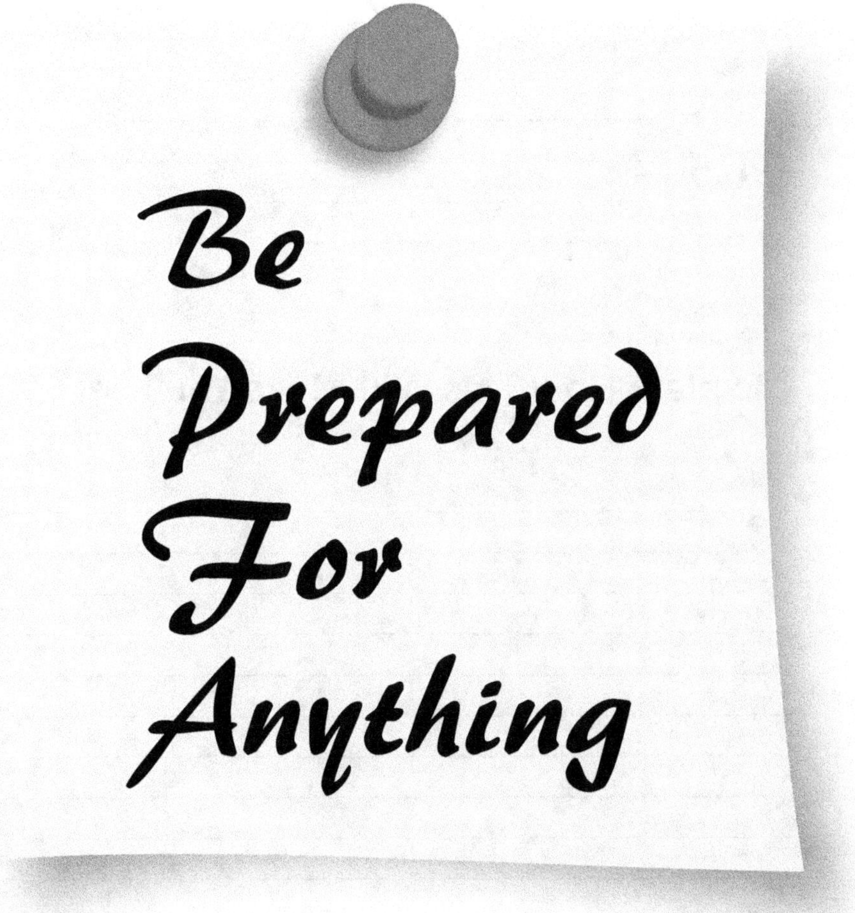
Be
Prepared
For
Anything

Write Down 5 LOVE QOUTES
THAT YOU THINK TODAY

1. _____
2. _____
3. _____
4. _____
5. _____

Explain How This Will Make You Feel

_____
_____
_____
_____
_____
_____
_____
_____
_____
_____

Today is

Sunday Monday Tuesday Wednesday Thursday Friday Saturday

2019

1 2 3 4 5 6 7 8 9 10 11 12 13 14 15 16 17 18 19 20 21 22 23 24 25 26 27 28 29 30 31

I'm feeling _____

_____

_____

_____

_____

_____

_____

_____

I'm thinking about...

My goals _____

_____

_____

_____

_____

_____

_____

_____

To Do List

Check	Task	Deadline
☐		
—		
☐		
—		
☐		
—		
☐		
—		
☐		
—		
☐		
—		
☐		
—		
☐		
—		

You Must LOVE YOURSELF FIRST

Picture of the day

Notes:

Additional Notes:

Additional Notes:

 # Health and Fitness Weekly Checklist

	M	T	W	TH	F	SA	SU
Drink 2L of water							
Workout for at least 30 minutes							
Stretch							
At least 5 servings of fruit/veg							
No eating after 9pm							
Try to get 8 hours of sleep							

Quick Checklist

What Should I Do

- [ ] _____
- [ ] _____
- [ ] _____
- [ ] _____
- [ ] _____

Notes

♥ My Parent Wish List ♥

- [ ] _____
- [ ] _____
- [ ] _____
- [ ] _____
- [ ] _____
- [ ] _____
- [ ] _____
- [ ] _____
- [ ] _____
- [ ] _____

Notes

Achievement ☀

- [ ] _____
- [ ] _____
- [ ] _____
- [ ] _____
- [ ] _____

Notes

Weekday To Do List

MONDAY

- ☐ _____
- ☐ _____
- ☐ _____
- ☐ _____
- ☐ _____

TUESDAY

- ☐ _____
- ☐ _____
- ☐ _____
- ☐ _____
- ☐ _____

WEDNESDAY

- ☐ _____
- ☐ _____
- ☐ _____
- ☐ _____
- ☐ _____

THURSDAY

- ☐ _____
- ☐ _____
- ☐ _____
- ☐ _____

FRIDAY

- ☐ _____
- ☐ _____
- ☐ _____
- ☐ _____
- ☐ _____

NOTES

- ☐ _____
- ☐ _____
- ☐ _____
- ☐ _____
- ☐ _____

Weekly To Do List

SATURDAY

- [ ] _____
- [ ] _____
- [ ] _____
- [ ] _____
- [ ] _____

SUNDAY

- [ ] _____
- [ ] _____
- [ ] _____
- [ ] _____
- [ ] _____

Notes

- [ ] _____
- [ ] _____
- [ ] _____
- [ ] _____
- [ ] _____

Journal

Date: _____

Topic:

_____

_____

_____

_____

_____

_____

_____

_____

_____

_____

_____

Share picture here:

If you can make a woman laugh, you can make her do anything

~ **Marilyn Monroe**